THE DAWN

of the

ROAR

THE LION'S VOICE

BERNICE ROSE

authorHOUSE®

AuthorHouse™
1663 Liberty Drive
Bloomington, IN 47403
www.authorhouse.com
Phone: 1 (800) 839-8640

Published by AuthorHouse 11/292017

ISBN: 978-1-5462-1672-8 (sc)
ISBN: 978-1-5462-1671-1 (e)

Not everyone has a heart big enough, those who have a big enough heart have reservations for people who they respect and people who they'll let in. People who don't have a very big heart will tend to put others beneath them and treat them as such, those are usually the people who wind up digging themselves into a hole so deep that they ask you to help them out of the hole but they forgot that they hurt you. The friends that the "Mean Girl's" in High School thought were their "Ride or die" friends weren't along for the ride anymore, in fact they got off the ride as soon as it needed a glitch fixed. That's what I learned about fake friends in high school, you have to make sure what kind of people you hang around, and if they like you for who you are or for who they thought they could treat you as. Narrowing down that process really sucks I know, you're going to have to learn the hard way sometimes, you're going to have to let go of the ones you've trusted so much in the past, but in the long run it'll pay off because you won't have to worry anymore about having friends who leave when the going gets tough. Now these people who actually think that people are beneath them have reservations when it comes to assigning different labels onto different individuals. So apparently, "The cool crew" of High school are thought to consist of the girls who feel as if everyone has a bad name because they're unique, so according to them, if you don't have grades like them you're stupid and if you go out with someone who one of them likes then you're a whore, if you are funny and not a size 2 then they say you are a joke just because not everyone wants to look like them. This is just the stereotype that Society has shaped, there are a whole lot more truly good people and not as many small hearted people out there, this is the experience that I know, but there will always be that one person who you grow so close to in High school that if you're lucky they might just ride with you until the wheels fall off. People are still going to overuse these labels, but it doesn't define who you are, it only defines who they are. I'm not saying it's not going to hurt at first, heck to the yeah it's going to hurt like hell and I think that many of us know that you might even feel like giving up some of the time, but all you need is one friend to tell you that you're worth it. Words really hurt, so when people in High School or out of High School say something hurtful to you you're going to cry, but don't hold it in because the tears that you don't let fall are going to seem like they're combining with all the other tears you've held back so far to form a ball of tears which just bursts out of our eyes one day and it hurts your heart. It'll feel like it's hard to breathe because you just keep crying, no matter how bad you want to stop crying the tears just don't stop coming out, so it's better to let the tears come down when they do come. Just because your crying doesn't mean you're not a role model, you crying just shows that you're human, what makes you a role model is what you do with the tears.

You can make it easier on yourself by taking the easy way out and planning on ending the pain, but that doesn't end the pain, it might pause it, but you're just going to exchange that pain for another type of pain which is you having the pain of not being able to see the day when you're happy, and the pain of knowing how much pain the fact you're not there anymore has caused your loved ones, yeah so you shouldn't do that, please don't do that. The better choice that actually really pays off is that after you cry you take those tears that you cried and let it lead you to the dream that you've always had and make a reality of it. It's weird to think that a masterpiece can come from tears, it can even sound really mean if you think of it in the wrong light, but if you read between the lines, you'll see that everything negative can be turned into a positive, even when the mirror is to fogged up with tears or fogged up because she was presenting a false reflection that the mirror couldn't recognize her. It's so easy to push away our loved ones when we're hurt for different reasons, maybe it's easy because pain had made it hard to trust anyone, maybe it's because you don't want to depend on anyone but you or maybe you just feel like your feelings are too deep for anyone to understand or simply because you feel like you venting to a loved one might bring them down with you. Some reasons are just unknown, but none of them do any good, if that person is really there for you, then you can push them out all you want but they're going to be right there when you feel like you're too broken to get back up.

Those "Mean Girls" in High School I was telling you about are probably going to be a big contribution of the people who judge you, call you names to your face, and make fun of you but other people are going to follow in their footsteps, sadly, but if you look at it in a positive way, you will see that you're doing something so right that it actually makes the mean crowd in high School want to waste their own time trying to bring you down and that time is wasted because you're too secure with who you are, little do you know that they're too insecure to leave you in the secure skin that you're in. I know it's extremely hard to ignore sometimes, but if you don't react then they're just left to deal with their own insecurities by themselves until they ask for help with it. Long story short, In the end it's the ones who've hurt you who will one day be able to see clear as day that they lost while they were trying to get you to lose what makes you YOU, but they lost when it came trying to get you to fail but you only succeeded. The only thing that matters and the thinking that you should always remember, something you're going to find out anyway, and here it is: No one has the power to fail you unless you give them that power, no matter the situation, you can't fail unless you want to fail. It's actually the truth that people who planned to make your life miserable empower themselves by accomplishing the task of making you cry, that's why you can't show them that of course it's going to hurt at first, because if you did even for a second, then they'll think that if they keep doing that same thing, then they'll think they can get you to see yourself as everything that they have said you are. Though that is their goal, you still get to decide, not everyone has a choice, but you will always have the choice to never let anyone diminish who you are, and that's a statement that's true in any situation, you will always be you. Nothing's wrong with being you, they might get you to believe that at times, but that doesn't mean anything's wrong with you, it means something's wrong with them, but they're too busy mocking you to deal with it. Judgementals are like bullies, in a way bullies and dogs are alike in the way that both dogs and bullies can sense fear, but the big difference between dogs and bullies is that dogs may jump up and lick you, most of them will not bite you, especially if you did nothing to them. Bullies are much different, when they sense fear equivalent to that of a dog, they bite you, but in the human sense bullies truly believe that they can honestly destroy you, but that is beyond impossible unless you let them.

The only one who can hurt you is you, sometimes we feel like we deserve to be hurt, it's kind of easy to slip into the dark place when you're too tired to fight. Most times we don't want to acknowledge that were not perfect, we can't be perfect so we beat ourselves up because we feel like there's something wrong with us, and we're lost for a while. Nobody's perfect though, that's a fact, there are people who seem to have everything together and seem to be living the greatest dream ever, but they went through times you have no idea about, times when they had thoughts that they couldn't do it. Even if its just for a minute, even if they feel like they're above you, they're definitely not perfect, but it's not a bad thing to not be perfect, not even close. I honestly can't imagine a world with everyone and everything being perfect, every single day you would have to follow the same daily routine and you could never talk about hard times without you feeling ashamed. It might just be me but I feel like having our battles and overcoming them just shows us how strong we are, especially when we have doubts and start thinking that we can't do it anymore, those are the moments that are the most powerful when we look back and think about how weak we thought we were and see how much we've overcome to get where we are. We all have something that keeps us together as individuals, for me it was my religion that held me together, for others it might be a dream they have in their head, their morals, or something else, a true friend that will stand by you and selflessly listens to you is really hard to find but is such a gift to have by your side, but what holds us this together as individuals is something that we in deep down in our soul that we hold so dear to our heart, a true friend comes pretty close to that, but we're always who we are before anyone came into the picture, so in the end we just have to remember who we are, and though it may take time to do we just have to love ourselves for it.

I remember something that she told me a wise woman once said to her, she said to her that she was living in God's body, so if she hurt herself with cuts, burns, pills that she didn't need, and all the things that she had done that did damage to her body, she was hurting God, and she just couldn't even start to imagine how she could hurt the one who made me who she actually was. When she heard that she then realized that what she was doing was basically a huge slap in God's face, she felt that she couldn't go on hurting who was and still is always there for her, so from then on she tried her very best to think twice before she did something that wasn't a very good choice. She'd learned that God will never give us more than we can handle, there were a whole bunch of times when she doubted that because she didn't feel like she could handle it anymore when it would keep being thrown at her, but once she had survived after that part of my battle was over, she had just found out that he just works in Mysterious ways. She thought that it was only me who knew me best and knew how much she could handle, but she didn't know there was someone who knew me better than me. Even if you're not a Christian I can still guarantee you that there's at least one person in your life who knows you better than you know yourself, it might be a parent or it might be a true friend or maybe both, but whoever they are they will hear you when you say you don't think you can do it anymore, but they know you'll pull through and they're rooting for you until the end of the ride. Just because you're feeling that way doesn't make you selfish, it means you're human and like Humans you bleed when you crash down, and you cry when you fall, some people don't understand that concept.

It doesn't make you a bad person if you lose yourself for a while as long as you find you in the end, you're not a bad person because you speak up instead of falling into silence. You don't have issues just because you want to be different, you're not crazy just because you live the way you want to live, you are not a bad role model because you cry when you're hurt, you are not going to lose just because they said you are. You are Human and only you can define you, people making fun of you defines them, you're someone completely different from who they make you feel like you are, they're only jealous people, jealous because your fine with being you, and being you is the only perfect that you can achieve, and it's more than enough perfect. The millions of songs that claim what doesn't kill you makes you stronger really makes a lot of sense because you don't die even though you feel like you might die because you've cried so many tears that your heart feels different, but you have experience in that tragedy so you won't fall as hard if you ever again experience anything like that situation, and you can feel yourself getting stronger every single time, you don't know how strong you are until you go through it. Life is full of tests like that, so after a while of battling obstacles in your life, taking on more challenges only makes you more determined, life is just a learning process, don't let it scare you away, just ace the test in your own way instead. Everyone has a different test in this life, so there's no answer that's right and no answer that's wrong, life is what you make it, so just make it your very own masterpiece, not everyone has to agree with it, it's between you and life.

There's only one life so forget about people who say you can't, they're too busy doubting you to live out their own test. Here's the way I see it: On the other hand, aside from being dogs, bullies actually can go by a better term called a "Vampires," they're vampires because they get pleasure from taking something from people, but the victims of this type of vampire can escape the vampire's grip at anytime, but they need the key to get out, the key is confidence. You need confidence to stop being a victim, if you don't have confidence then you're going to believe that you are everything that the vampires say you are, but all they say are a bunch of lies, because you're way better than what they say. Even though you don't see it at that moment, you already have so much confidence because you're not so insecure that you had to go and kick someone to the ground just to make yourself feel better, you just need to find that confidence that you always had inside you, once you do that, no one can stop you. It's easy to slip into that dark space and believe what they're saying until you just give up, but it's not easy to say "No," and fight your way out with all you have, I don't mean physically, because that's exactly what they want, if you physically hurt them they probably won't smile at first, but in the end they smile because they can still get under your skin. If you physically fight that bully, then they're satisfied with what they did to you, even if you win, as soon as those bruises heal, they'll watch you and smile at what they've done, because while you feel like you've escaped their grip, you've allowed them to turn you into who you never thought you'd be, now you have a whole new mindset that's negative and now you let that bully make you insecure like they were, and chances are you're either going to become that bully or you are going to become a worst bully, or even your own bully. Don't let that bully change you because you won't recognize who you see in the mirror anymore, let that bully be their own enemy, but you don't have time for enemies. Making your bullies your enemies only gives them your time which they don't deserve to have the pleasure of claiming, they can be their own enemy until they realize that there's no point of fighting an enemy when sometimes you have to fight through the obstacles of life, life is too short to give undeserving people your time, you just gotta keep pushing on because you might miss a moment that's actually worth your time.

We all have different parents, some are great and don't have many flaws, but being a parent is hard and parents don't always the answers, Parents are humans at the end of the day, their kids are humans, sometimes Humans gotta help each other, when parents aren't right their kids might help them figure it out instead of getting as irritated as some parents can get you. Who really has time to hold anger or hatred for anyone inside of them? I understand that some parents shouldn't even have the name of a parent, but unless you forgive them, they're always going to come back in some way to get under your skin, and not by showing up on your doorstep, but by the little things that random people will do that will remind you of them somehow, or maybe because you heard something that you know they would've said, but whatever it is, they're memory is going to come back to mess with you.

So just forgive them, it's not as easy as only saying "Just forgive them," Forgiving anyone who's done anything ever to hurt you is really hard, because it seems like you're letting them off the hook, but you'll only be showing them that they can't hurt you anymore. Forgiveness isn't for them it's for you, you forgiving them sets you free because holding back Hatred for someone else in your heart makes your heart darker over time, you control your own heart and your own feelings, that's the one thing that they can't control, you are in charge of your own life and destiny. Those people don't deserve to control or change the part of you that makes you, and I'm not saying it doesn't take time, it takes a lot of time to be that kind of "Ok" as a person. When you are O.K with you as a person, then If I were you I would forgive them because hate take too much time and they deserve to see that the pain behind your eyes will go away because you said enough is enough. I knew this girl whose Father always said she was nothing, had no college potential, would never amount to anything, and would always compare her to everyone she knew who had big things happening in their lives at the moment, she felt like she had to become those people so she could make him proud.

Little did she know that she didn't have to change who she was to make someone else proud, if they knew how to be proud of you then you being who you are would always be more than enough. If they can' t be proud of you for who you are but they're more content with you if you pretend to be someone else, then they weren't really worth trying to make proud in the first place. The fact that you trusted that person enough to try to make that person proud just shows how big your heart is for wanting their approval that much, but when you try to make someone proud and they like you for you, then you don't even try, you just have to be the you that you always were at heart. There are some people who will do wrong by you and instead of apologizing to you they will buy you some kind of gift and feel as if that makes everything all better, that's the kind of parent's that this girl knew, so she didn't really grow up in a family that talked about anything but the positive, at least not where she was concerned. It was pretty much as if she didn't deserve to be able to cry because she was being selfish and her cries were actually called "Manipulative" by someone who was supposed to be close to her, 2 people actually, it hurt her because she used to be really close to one of them, she started depending on herself, it was just easier and she knew that she would never let herself down. Those are the kind of situations that make it a little harder to trust, I guess it's hard to trust anyone who you've trusted with a lot after they've done nothing but prove you wrong in trusting them. She knew people who held onto revenge like a rock and fed off of the hurt and all the tears of other people, what hurt her was that some of those people were close to her.

Those people all will realize one day that diamonds, rubies, pearls, big houses, Chanel bags, Gucci and all the rest of the finest material in the world will never be a true apology unless they say the actual words and acknowledge what they've done, if they don't know what they've done and they still try to apologize, then it's not an apology, it's just them telling you what you want to hear, she could have told herself what she wanted to hear, She would rather just hear the truth from other people.

People usually wind up thinking that D.N.A makes a family, but D.N.A can walk out the door and out of your life whenever things start to get tough, that doesn't mean that there aren't people with your D.N.A Who love you. Love makes the best family, Love that is unconditional, that's the most true kind of love and luckily that kind of love comes with looking out for the best for you always. Unconditional love comes with Unconditional support but also not encouraging you to make the wrong decisions that might break your heart, of course we have to make our own decisions and learn on our own, but real love will make sure that we don't make a decision that will ruin our life and ultimately stop us from being able to make more of our own decisions on our own, which would happen if we made the wrong decision when it was life changing to make the right one. Parents are humans, just like us, that doesn't mean everyone is meant to be a parent, but the ones who are the ones who protect you. My point is that you can't just show up out of the blue one day and just yell out that you're a parent when you haven't even been in that kid's life, love makes a parent, not D.N.A. So it doesn't matter if it's a Foster Parent, a Step-parent, or your biological parent, if they love you in the way where they're actually there for you, really there for you, and that doesn't mean that they're just in your life for the wrong reasons, but if they're really there for you then they're the right type of parents for you. One more thing, a parent is someone you are comfortable enough around, a foster parent or a Step parent becomes a real parent if you're comfortable enough to let them in and if they accept you for who you are always and love you unconditionally, then they're a parent, that's the definition of a parent, love and approval of who you are no matter what. Even when you get in an argument with that parent, that doesn't mean their love for you goes away, unconditional love doesn't run away when the going gets tough, unconditional love gets mad like Human beings do, but remembers that they love you and when you need them, they're there even if we really messed up. Parents are after all human beings, and sometimes they need a shoulder to cry on too, they can still relate to us. It's a Heaven sent gift for anyone to parent a child, and it's a heaven sent gift for us to have the right type of parents in our lives, that's not everyone, but if we do find them, then they're a blessing for us to have and we're a blessing for them to have.

There are the wrong type of parents are out there, and a lot of people with real nerves who will butt in and tell you that you're being ungrateful, but that's not their place. She used to get so angry and furious because so many people kept telling her how to act and who to be like, but they didn't know anything that happened when they weren't looking, they kept saying she was being disrespectful only because she didn't act like a princess or like everybody else. I'm 100% sure that all of them had moments that they weren't proud of in their lives, but it's criticism that they would try to force me to live exactly lie they wanted me to, oh well, you can't always win. It took her a while to fully understand that you can't win in everybody's eyes, if you make someone happy by changing something about you then you make someone else angry because you changed yourself to get their approval, in any situation no matter what it is you can't win with everybody, so just win for yourself.

You can't win with everyone because you're always going to have haters in life, if you don't have hater's in life then you're not doing something right, if you have Hater's all that means is that they're mad because everyone wants to get the prize and go to the top before you so they can be first place in their eyes, but just because someone is not exactly that person who got to the top, doesn't mean that they're not going to get there and they might even already be there. Hater's want to stop you from getting to the top, but if you keep pushing to the top despite what they say then your Hater's don't hate as much because they're wasting their hate on someone who doesn't fight it back with hate, because Hate fought with hate makes a dead end, but if you take Hatred as something to keep you determined to prove the hate wrong, then you'd be fighting Hate with love which makes a fire of determination that burns too bright to be the color of hate. Hater's are people who don't have to hate just to win, but they think it makes a difference, hating just stops you from having all the good times that you can have if you just let go of jealousy. No matter what anyone says, it's never too late to make things right and win, Life's way too short to hold grudges but just long enough to right your wrongs and become exactly the version of the you who you want to be.

Some parents feel like their children are cattle, sorry for the harsh title, what it means is some parents feel like their children are their territory. Children are individual human beings that can't be controlled, no human being should be controlled, they should definitely be controlled when they cross the line, and let's be super honest a lot of us need to be told sometimes! No one should be treated like territory, we all have feelings even though some of us would rather not show the parts of us that aren't too happy, like I said before just because you're not happy that doesn't mean you're bringing the person you love sadness that makes them wish that they never asked you what was wrong that day. Real friends will listen to you and care about what you're going through and the only reason that it might seem like it makes them sad is because they want you to be happy, not just a true friend, but everyone who loves you cares. Those people who only stick with you when you're happy aren't really friends you're going to want to keep. It's so irritating when you yourself would be willing to listen to anything your friends would say no matter how they feel but yet they would not do even close to that for you, it's devastating, but I've learned over the years that friends stop being your friends not always because you did anything, but because those people are not meant to be in the next chapter of your life. Even if the right type of friendship where you had a true friendship, both you and that person will find your way back into each other's lives and that's how you will both know who is meant to be in your life and exactly is not.

CHAPTER 1
SCARS

Someone might think a scar will fade and they might say that you will get over it, but there's a difference between a bruise and a scar, bruises physically hurt while scars remind you of the hurt and sorrow without you physically having to hurt. Scars never fade but bruises won't stay, Scars can get in your way if you let them control you by you not forgiving that scar for making its mark on your skin. That scar hurts more than bruises ever could because scars are only memories that hurt until you learn to let go of the hatred of that memory, that doesn't mean that you forget that memory. Scars are deep and therefore, hard to forgive but each second that you don't forgive a scar for being with you the scar tissue only deepens, and the bruise fades way faster than the scar's pain but the scar can't hurt you if it doesn't hold your hate underneath it.

Some people just don't understand scars, it really hurts because you would help wipe away their scars.

People don't understand when you hurt but that doesn't mean that you need those people to understand you, you need people who love you and if they do love you then don't really need to understand you in order to say the things that'll help you, it just kind of comes naturally to those who care. Scars heal but they need time to go away, we all have scars that will always be shown to us and won't disappear, but those scar stay with us because they remind us of our strength. We don't have to feel strong in order to be strong, a lot of times we're being strong just because we keep pushing through the right way even though it's really hard. One version of how to scar a child is to leave their lives before they're even before they're born, because when they find out about you eventually then they feel like it's their fault. It's not their fault, but it hurts them even more if you wait a bunch of years before you enter their lives, especially for the second time, it's kind of ripping off a bandage, the longer you wait to pull it off, the higher the chances of that bandage coming off and really hurting you.

She tried to wipe away every scar that she could but it wasn't in the question to forgive at that very moment, she wouldn't forgive because she wouldn't open her heart in fear that it wasn't done healing and it would go right back to breaking if she didn't keep her guard around it. She couldn't see past the depth of the scar long enough to learn at that very moment how and why she could let go of the strong feelings she had behind that scar. She felt like she could get past everything that scar represented without forgiving who or what made that scar, but no matter how long she could go on without feeling the pain of that scar, as soon as she looked back at the scar the memories would just flood back to her all at once. Her not having forgiveness for that scar only hurt her although she thought that forgiving meant that what made her scar would be free if she didn't hold that over their heads anymore, but who-ever made that scar would know how wrong what they did was, but if she forgave them then they would both be free although that person who made the scar would see the error of their ways no matter how free they were, if they were wrong then they would feel it dawn on them the minute you forgave them. That doesn't mean that they would be miserable forever because of it, but you wouldn't be miserable because you wouldn't be dwelling on the hurt but instead you'd see past it to what lesson you learned from it while that person would know what they did wrong, if you don't forgive then you live inside that scar trying to mold it into something that it can't ever be and that alone will be enough to srive you crazy simply because the scar is built under your skin and you can't seem to control it.

Even if your biological parent didn't know about you before, it still really hurts and you probably have so many questions about why they've found you when you did even if it's not their fault because they didn't know about you. You usually end up being angry at one of your parents, but honestly it's kind of a weird situation because that gap in your life hurts you either way even if you don't show it. That situation can make you stronger if you handle it the right way, and no one can really tell you exactly how to handle that situation, but you'll end up doing the right thing eventually in good time, that's just the way it works. No matter what happens the point of this advice is that you should never let anyone doubting you stop you from doing you, always do you, it doesn't matter what anyone thinks YOU matter and that's all you need. What I want to say to those parents though is just leave if you don't want to be there for them, it doesn't hurt them honestly it hurts you because they're going to rise to the top regardless, it's just a matter of whether or not you want to be there to witness where their journey takes them and there's no coming into their lives just because they made it. Money may be an extremely wanted want, but it's not a need, because the human heart and soul were both made long before money ever came into the picture, a creation is heaven sent, money is man-made.

Human being's feel so many emotions daily, their understanding is amazing but some people just don't use that gift, but the personalities to the lack of understanding in people are definitely interesting, some people have just been hurt so much that they don't realize how much they hurt others when they are reflecting off of what had happened to them. Those who have big hearts realize how they were acting a short while later. Ruthless people always just dismiss they're behavior because they mostly just don't show that they feel, because it makes them more open to get hurt again, that's how we think. I hate that Men don't feel like they can cry because it makes them weak, that's how all Men think but that's far from the truth. It's great and courageous that Men feel like they need to always be so strong because they feel like it's both unattractive and it makes them look bad, but all it means is that you don't want to bottle it up and that you're not afraid of anything plus it makes you really understanding. Anyone who ever bottles up their tears or other feelings then one day it'll just be too much to handle and all you'll see is black and you never want to get to that place, it's no fun and doesn't help anything. It would be great if Men actually showed their feelings and didn't feel like they weren't strong, girls are strong too, but Men hold it together even if they cry.

That's when the scars heal, when you let them out, and a therapist shouldn't be the only one who listens, but even if a friend won't listen, at the end of the day you still made it on your own. Don't be afraid to see a therapist, it doesn't make you weak when you reveal your scars. You are a beautiful soul always, even when you can't find it, just because you can't see it doesn't mean it's not real, Confidence takes you further than you know, I have bad days a lot but when I'm confident and I tell the voices in my head to shut up, when anyone sets their mind to something, no matter what they can't be stopped. You just have to want it bad enough then it'll take some time but there is no doubt what-so-ever that you will better than alright soon enough. Once you tell those voices that enough is enough then it's at that moment that you can finally leave all the doubts, fears, hatred, and all the negatives behind. Those scars can't hurt you anymore, even if you forgive you can't forget, but you can definitely move on from those times. I'm not saying that it's going to be easy because it's not, but you're not free until you do, even if you choose to believe that you are. Forgive for you and for no one else, you forgive them but that doesn't mean that you're letting them off the hook, that means your scars get lighter and go away sooner because everything they say or do doesn't get under your skin to deepen your scars because you let the negative things go in one ear and out the other. The thing is that a lot of people in life bully or not, they want to see you crash down when you're doing good but they were doing just fine when you were down, but you see you need haters because Human beings have this drive in them where they just want to prove the haters wrong for doubting them. The more successful you get at whatever you do, the more haters that you're going to have, it's just the world that we live in today, but it's fine because it sparks Determination. So many demons that haunt us stop us from Finding success, but we shake all of them off and see an Angel then prove them wrong. The feeling's amazing, scars that hurt us to the bone are no more, we only see happiness at that moment, I know it seemed impossible to be happy at the time, but it makes you're proud that you beat the past. It's a super powerful feeling when you prove to your hater's that you weren't what they said about you, you were way better. I remember this one bully that she had in high school who started mocking her because she spoke with a speech impediment and she actually had the absolute nerve to tell her that she could barely speak English let alone Spanish. The teacher in that class couldn't care less, but that was the first time that she realized that her speech impediment was so visible, and besides that a schoolmate of hers said that he would shoot himself in the head if she could walk in a straight line across the handball court, all she could think of was why me?" She just couldn't figure out exactly why she had been given this balance problem let alone a speech impediment that people made fun of, she wasn't even "supposed" to be diagnosed with Ataxia and Celiac disease (Celiac disease is an allergy to all Gluten which throws your balance off even more if you eat Gluten), her doctor told her that it was normally found in Europeans, it was so frustrating because it made it so much harder to do everyday things. She got to do an 8 count dance routine while the rest of the dance club did the entire dance which was way more than 8 counts and all because she couldn't twirl. She fell in the mud 5 or 6 times probably throughout one year because the path to go to my classes was extremely narrow, and that probably happened each year that she went to that High school, and she went there for 3 years, her senior year all the boys who made fun of her balance were standing at the top of the path laughing at me because she fell off the path and got her pants all muddy, then they all got mad because she told her biology teacher that they laughed at her. She had to leave school early all the days that she fell off that path, it didn't really physically hurt her when she fell down, it only hurt her emotionally, she just could never really understand how human beings could walk so perfectly, she realized exactly how perfectly and more clearly realized it as soon as she went to an airport and every person who walked by me asked her if she needed help or if she was okay every single step that she would take, She thought to herself "Am I really that bad?" She didn't ask for this disease or the stupid diagnosis or to not be able to dance without falling down and she definitely didn't ask to fall down unexpectedly and have everyone laugh at her because they hadn't seen too many people with Atazia in their lives. She didn't ask Policemen and Police women to stop her 5 times because she looked like she was drunk, the police had the nerve to stop her and ask her what Ataxia was, they had never heard about it before and they had the nerve to stop her because she didn't walk normally. She went into a few bars in her life when she turned 21 years old, every single bartender who she ran into except for one, all concluded that she already had enough to drink because she walked the way that she did. She didn't ask for it so she didn't know why she had received it, she didn't ask to speak different than "Normal" and she didn't ask to be bullied, she didn't ask for her head to almost explode because stupid people decided to act stupid.

Before she turned 21 years old and she couldn't drink she would stuff her face with food because she was bored or sad or so happy that she felt like she didn't deserve to be, she just took the pain away with food. She was hurt and she was angry, she felt stupid and she felt like she was weak because she wasn't "Normal." Who wants to be normal though? I don't think I'd want to be "Normal" even if I could be, I love being unique even when no one understands why, because if they don't understand me then they won't understand how much worth of mine is going to be visible one day and they can't say anything about it because they couldn't see it and they didn't believe in it. She just kept saying to herself "Thank God I can drink at age 18 in London." She went to London during the summer of 2016 and 2017, of course in 2017 she was 21 already, and it was the best feeling being temporarily blacked out, but that's the keyword, temporary, it never lasts. She didn't care though, as far as she was concerned she was 21 and would drink every time things weren't as pretty as they used to be to her. She didn't see that Alcohol would one day kill her, but She kind of really hoped that it would, besides she'd done so much toxic stuff to her body in the past that she was confident that it would all re-surface very soon and end it all. I won't tell you all the things she had done in the past because I don't want to give you any ideas but it's a long list, pain is not a competition, I can't stand people who think it is a competition. She just kept wishing that she had finally broke her glasses.

CHAPTER 2
BROKEN GLASSES

She tried so hard to squint while she couldn't see a glimpse of anything but fog through her glasses, it wasn't her eyesight that was the problem, but is was merely the fact that she felt enough to let hatred become the reason that she couldn't see that much of anything that she used to. She'd wished she could've broken her glasses on some days, because her glasses got so fogged up that she could barely even see. Crying so much gives you a headache and she didn't have time for it. So when she got her first good paying job she was so determined to rent a room somewhere else, of course that was a few months after she started working there. It was still dark, but she was thankful to have a job, because she didn't want to be in that house longer than she needed to be. house longer than I needed to be. She knew that she needed to stop cutting because it wasn't fair to her, because even though both her and her demons didn't feel like she deserved to be happy and they both felt like she should have pain and not be happy. That's the problem though, we sometimes think the worst of ourselves, but we shouldn't let our demons win because they've never really done anything for us have they? We feel like they have done at least something for us because the cuts and burns took our pain away, but it was all temporary. Doing bad things doesn't solve anything for a long amount of time, just for a little while, we just gotta think positive even in the hardest situations. It's Cleeshae I know, but I say you should think positive because what else can you do if you're tired of the pain? Really we can make cuts so deep that we don't even recognize who we see in the mirror anymore, but what does the result do? You can spend the time you're using to do that and instead try to make yourself happy, easier said than done I know, but I do know because I went through it, no one deserves to lose themselves like that. There's really no right or wrong way to go through the process of finding yourself, and just because you lost who you are for a while doesn't mean you're abnormal, you're not weird you're not crazy, you might feel like you're going to go crazy, but you're not going to. You just gotta calm down, put a vision in your head of what kind of version of You you want to be, and go for it, you can't really fail yourself. Failures are still masterpieces in the making, you just can't see them yet, not at first at least, only because you're way too focused on the part where you messed up that you can't the parts that are beautiful, those parts are there and no matter who you are there are beautiful parts I can promise you that.

At one point in time she got to a point where she reached her ultimate point of frustration, she was frustrated with everything, she was frustrated with the fact that she held on to so much hate but she didn't want to hate, but the biggest frustration that she held inside was the frustration that she couldn't do a thing about it. She never felt so weak, as weak as that moment when she threw her glasses on the ground watching it fall apart from it hinges, the ironically funny part about that was the fact that she felt like that symbolized how her life was falling apart at the hinges, but throwing her glasses away for a while didn't do her any harm. Honestly she was just tired of wiping away the fog off of her glasses from all the tears every 5 minutes, so she took them off, I have no idea what would've happened if she had contacts on. Therefore, she stuck to wearing glasses, besides, she wore glasses from the beginning and she would feel comfortable enough taking her glasses along for the journey with her because they did after all witness all the tears that she cried so she wanted the broken glasses to be a souvenir to look back on when she finished living out this chapter.

Even though it was too dark to see a lot of the hidden words of wisdom around her there was one thing that she could see, she knew deep, deep down that she would eventually close this chapter of her life, and by eventually she meant soon because deep down she could feel her heart getting weaker and close to its breaking point. Sure she would complain a lot and say that the pain was too much a lot of times, but her heart was the one that knew her exact breaking point and her mind was the one that lied and made her feel like she couldn't do it anymore, but she knew honestly that she would get through it somehow because she could only see pulling through as her only option because if she made taking the easy way out a possible option then she probably would've considered it as the easier option. That would have tempted her and when she was tempted to do something it was usually really hard to not do it, so she steered away from the thought, besides, a couple years have passed since she had entered into the slum that she was currently in so she got to a point where she wanted to at least start to try to find a puzzle piece that would help her find the missing message of the rest of the puzzle.

She wasn't going to go into that situation where she would let them dig that hole and push her into it like every time before, she went into that situation knowing that there was a big chance that they would be immature and just dismiss her from even starting to make her point, but she didn't care. They scarred her so many times before but she was used to it by that time, she learned to never let them see her cry because if she did let them make her cry then they wouldn't stop until she gave up, so she wasn't going to let them have that power over her where they knew how much she cared so they took advantage of that, so she went there with a stone heart. She could make herself so ice cold that someone could feel how cold and rock hard the ice was just by walking near her, she could be so guarded that the armor she was wearing would be so many walls that you could barely even see my face, and she could wear so many masks that people could forget that the real her ever existed. The only reason that she felt that way was because she let them make her feel that, she had only heard what those people told her for so many years and she didn't really think too much about if what they told her was right or if it was wrong, it was just what they said and she never questioned it before because she didn't feel like it led her wrong before. The point is that she had allowed them to distract her so much that she dropped her flashlight so far down that it literally took her years and years to get back and even when she got it back she still had to change out the fuse more than most flashlight fuses need to be changed. Someone who is not you should never have the power to change you and should definitely Never EVER have the power to ruin you no matter how bad you feel about yourself or about that situation, and the sad thing is that sometimes people just find that it's easier to throw out the flashlight and so they gave that person that flashlight and now that person can never use that flashlight again because the person who gave up that flashlight thought that they couldn't turn on the flashlight no matter what they did, but they were thinking with their mind at that point, they were just listening to their instinct. Their minds were working with the bully who stole the flashlight, their minds were working against them but not for bad reasons, their mind is there so they can get determined to prove it wrong, their heart is what is going to tell them that they can handle what is coming up next.

We can hide it really well though can't we? We can just paint a smile on our face and it's like we have a paper bag on our face and we just drew on it to make it look happy, any of us can wear a mask and no one would ever know because that specific person might have trust issues or might feel like the whole world is against us or feel as if they're a burden. You're not a burden, whoever you are you're a gift that no one took the time to see, and that's not fault because they didn't see you, it's their fault because they never had the sense to open their eyes because they slept while you were standing right there. We should all open our eyes more because someone can smile one second then be gone the next and we wish we could take back what we said or did but it's too late for that now, it messes with you if you did something you regret and can't see them to apologize or make it better because they're not there anymore, so there's no way to make up for it anymore. You can't cry and try and hide it, you can't say "It's allergies" and shake it off you can't just say nothing's wrong because if you hold back your tears then people can see right through you and tell that something's wrong, someone who doesn't care is just going to ask you if you're okay and leave your side just because you said one or two words. Someone who cares about you is going to stay and care about why you're hurting, because anyone who loves you can see right through you, that doesn't mean you're a burden that means they don't want to see you cry but fake friends ask how you're doing as a casual question but stop caring when you're not happy. I'm not saying if the friend can't tell that you're unhappy they're a bad friend, I'm not saying that at all, because a lot of times it's not obvious but you only hide your scars for so long before someone sees them, and that doesn't just mean someone who knows you, a stranger can walk up to you and become your true friend but you won't know that until they help you. She let herself think that way and she let herself accept the picture of what everyone else wanted her to think she was, she told herself that she deserved to feel as dark as she did because she wasn't happy in so long that Sadness became her safe place. Hatred sucks, it makes people bitter, so bitter that you forget who really are and you stoop to the level of the people who hurt you. What you're doing is you're giving those people the control that you have over yourself and now they can make you a different darker person until you're too far gone, and you were at one time a happy you who didn't let anything define yourself but now your letting someone else define you. Let go of hatred because until you do you're basically a prisoner to that person, so She knew firsthand that It's really hard, but you gotta be the bigger person and show them that they never had the power over you that they thought had, and they're always going to try to break you but once you stop them by showing them that you're done being the victim then they stop trying eventually and focus on being a better person because they can't win at that game so they'll play the right kind of game. So you're actually helping them move on, sadly it's at your expense but it's not at your expense if you don't let it be. I realize this is all easier said than done, it's especially going to sound really cleeshae while you're going through it yourself, but one day when you find this outlook helpful and you can take this outlook and finish your masterpiece. Once you find the flashlight in the dark it'll be really easy to see how beautiful the masterpiece is and once you see that the possibilities of how far you can take the masterpiece in life can't ever be defined because it'll leave you speechless, it might not seem that way now but what I mean is you don't really believe all that you're capable of until you achieve it all. Don't get me wrong you don't have to achieve the dream you have just to prove that you have it with you, what I mean is you never fully realize how many blessings that you have until you sit back and watch your life just unravel into the beautiful masterpiece that you always envisioned in your head. The very first second that you realize that you've made your dream a reality and you can actually see it as clear as a masterpiece in an Art Gallery which is exactly what it will be, and you realize all that you've done to make it to that point in your life, you'll be speechless at first, there's no telling exactly what you'll do to express the feeling of all the pride you have in that moment while you finally can see all the things that you've worked so hard for finally pay off. In that specific moment you will feel like it was just yesterday that you started working on your masterpiece and overnight it finished and you're standing before it, when it actually sinks in that you've made the dream a reality, it will playback in your mind and show you exactly how hard you've worked and what phases and obstacles you've passed through to get where you really needed to be. In that flash back you will see all the times you've cried, all the times you've messed up, all the times you've wanted to give up everything, all the times you just feared what would happen when you achieved your dream, and look at the result and be satisfied exactly where you're sitting at that moment.

A Lot of people have that problem where they're afraid of their success because they happen to see someone who turned into a completely different person for the worst because the success that they've found had gotten to their heads and misled them to take it too far, but just because they took that path that doesn't mean that it will be your same path. Whether or not that person was misled by their success, the harsh reality of it is that that person allowed their success to define who they are as a person, you define who you are, dreams are one of the world's greatest qualities and gifts of life, but the thing is you define your big dream, it doesn't define you. Don't lose who you are as a person when you get to where you always wanted to be because the person whom you would've been leaving behind if you did that, would just disappear and one day you might not be able to find the "Real" you anymore, you might lose yourself for good if you let success change you. That doesn't mean you're them, you're not going to crash down just because someone else did, they're not you, you are who you feel like you need to be.

Own your dream don't let your dream own you, if you don't want to end up like them then don't do what they did, it's honestly that simple, don't do what you see them do and you'll be fine, just be you, no one else because a million of that person can never be you and you are beautiful no matter what. Me, myself, I would honestly most likely cry the day I achieved all that I wanted and needed to be, just because I'm an emotional person (and quite honestly I'm a bit of cry baby), but that doesn't mean that you're a cry baby just because you don't believe how far you've come, that just means you've put everything you had into your dream and it paid off, finally, and being speechless means that you can cry. The bruises that you had from the past all fades away but the scars will always be there to remind you of where you were, where you are, and where you are going, so you keep the scars to show you which route you can't take anymore, the scars mean you've let go of what can't be there anymore but you learned how to knock the bruises out.

Scars are tricky because sometimes it's easy to let it bring back a bruise, some bruises are easy to want again mostly because you're just not ready to believe that you don't deserve the tears anymore. It's easy to crawl back in that hole that you've made if it didn't close completely closed in the first place and don't let anyone tell you that you're making it up or that you just want attention, it doesn't matter the reason, and it doesn't matter who doesn't believe it. At the end of the day you know you and it hurts because the people close to you who were there when you were going through the ups in your life just decided that they didn't want to ride with you because you changed for the worst. Friends grow apart yeah but if they're not there anymore it's a heck of a sting I know, but soon enough you will see that it was cool having them as a friend for a while but they were never meant to ride with you until the end.

I may sound harsh when I say that, but I'm saying that because it's just the way that this life goes, our lives have many segments, pages and chapters to it, and not everyone's meant to be in the next part of your life with you. I don't believe the saying that some people weren't built to have that big of a heart to take on a friend's baggage, I believe that certain people weren't made to fit the missing puzzle piece to your jigsaw puzzle in life. It can be a real blessing to have had those people in your life in the first place, most of the time you can look back on your memories together and think on a time where you were glad that that person was in your life at that time. Now that doesn't mean that you need that person to be in your life again, it just means that it wasn't all bad, plus you just got another big life lesson and that means that you'll be ready and have the knowledge that it takes to take the next life lesson that life throws at you, because you'll have a few more of those lessons thrown at you.

You can handle them all without a doubt, it just all works out in the end, no one really knows how but you're always okay in the end but you have to hold on, and then you can look back one day soon enough and see that you made the right choice.

CHAPTER 3
OUTLETS

F ood was still her outlet for so long, she was almost sure that she kicked that habit a while ago, but when she couldn't drink Alcohol because her parents didn't allow her to live under their roof if she even drank one beer as far as they could tell. The thing about binge eating for her was that even when she didn't feel like she wanted the food, it was like there was a force pulling her towards the food, she knew the negative outcomes that Binging that meal would bring, but she only thought of the space that she was in at that moment, instead of looking ahead at the long-term consequences, that was just her headspace back then. Alcohol was a step up from binge-eating for her personally just because Alcohol allowed her to forget, at least for a little while, it might be an ugly side of people who drink Alcohol for the wrong reasons, but we don't really care how ugly we seem, more how we feel. Alcohol is probably one of the only things that actually allowed her to forget everything she was becoming and everything that she'd heard and seen during her lifetime.

People may have said that she was being selfish and ungrateful because a lot of people in her life cared and wanted to hear what she had to say but all the fake people in her life subtracted themselves out of my life the very second that she stopped being so happy, and they didn't even have the respect to say it to her face. In my opinion, when you see someone going through hard times and you were at one time close to that person, no matter how close, then you should be able to have the respect for what that person is going through and that respect is letting that person know if you're just going to let them be who they are without you. I think that hurts no matter what but eventually that person will understand and appreciate that you let them know instead of just staying when you didn't care enough to physically be there when they needed you there. That's when that person learns how much they resent you, because in their mind you sat there and laughed while they cried and they could only see that you were there, so just respect people enough to tell them the truth. She was eating too much not because she was just that hungry, She was eating because she was bored and sometimes because she was thinking too much, when she ate more than her stomach could handle the food seemed to form a ball inside that seemed to numb me out of feeling like she was about to go crazy and it seemed to stop my emotions from spiraling out of control.

Even when she did binge eat, it was bitter-sweet, she felt good and bad but at different times, she felt good at first eating the food because it was her distraction when she didn't want to focus, but on the other hand she knew that taking her emotions out on food wasn't getting her anywhere, it was just blocking her from going into the real world and handling things the way an Adult should. It was actually really an addiction, Binge-eating really was an escape that some people really need, or at least they feel like they really need it, just like Alcohol it is just temporary. We would sometimes think if we did it enough then it could be a permanent feeling, but we don't realize that it comes at such a high price, that price is your health, and you letting food control you. Even though alcohol is very different from food because Alcohol is toxic to the body it's still the same concept, it's your personal escape that comes at a price. Now we're okay with that price at first because the pain just gets too much to bare and those escapes take the pain away for a second, and then we read the fine print, and that leads us to recognize exactly what the pain manifested into. We didn't realize that when we signed up for an escape plan, we signed up for its side effects and everything else that came with it, we don't see the damage done until it's done and all laid out right in front of our faces, and it's too late. It's never too late for help though, just make sure to get it before everything in you breaks down, hopefully it won't come to that, but what's crazy is that we have no idea how far we actually escaped when we did, we just know that we escaped for a little while only when things got really bad, we didn't realize that the damage could be permanent.

She had come to a place in her life where she had to choose between binge-eating to escape from life or drinking to forget everything else. She didn't remember how much people would look at her everywhere she went because of how much she was over-eating; she hadn't felt as if many people had stared at her for eating excessively in public for a while. It just felt weird to her and like she couldn't really find the reasoning to why she started up that routine again, and she couldn't relate to different things as she did in her past such as music which saved her life, and the only thing that was clear to her was that she wasn't the girl who she used to be.

After she got some sleep she came to the conclusion that she was driving herself crazy and over-thinking partly because she was aspiring to do a lot in her life at that point, but she had to just sit back and take a breath to clear her mind. She couldn't clear her head, she tried to clear her mind an excessive amount of times before but nothing was clear about what went on in her head, she couldn't stop to take a breath because if she did then all that would happen would be her living every second saying "What if?" It wasn't fun living like that because when she use to think that way she thought of really big "What if's" and other really big questions like "So what?" Those questions would just play so much racket in her head that it would lead her down dark and twisted paths until she lost her flashlight again, she couldn't let herself take her there again because it wasn't fair to her or to everything she'd ever known. So she piled a bunch of work on top of each other so that she didn't have time to think, but believe it or not she was doing all that because she felt like she felt like she was on her way to being happy, don't get me wrong mentally she was a lot better than she used to be, but there was still a missing puzzle piece in her life. She just couldn't find what it was, she knew that what was missing was her being truly happy, but she just wasn't sure exactly how her happiness looked like, she had no idea what image to look for where she was happy the whole time, but she figured that it would just hit her one day out of the blue and besides she didn't really have time to track it down, so she was alright being the "okay" that she was at the moment for now. The only way that she stayed encouraged was by her thinking to herself that everytime she felt a storm raging over her there would only be a brighter rainbow each time, and whenever it would really pour the rainbow would almost look so 3D that she could actually feel like she was actually living in the rainbow itself, way better than the movies.

She realize how ridiculously corny that sounded but its true depending on what way you look at it, now that doesn't mean that you'll live on an actual rainbow and on the end is a pot of gold, but metaphorically speaking every part of that statement is true. The battles that you fight on your days when you feel like the world is defeating you, those days symbolize the storm and when you make it through that the storm that's when you can see the rainbow which is the day that you don't feel as down as the day that you felt that, and the pot of gold at the end of the rainbow represents the amount of happiness that you'll have at the end of all your battles. There's a pot of gold at the end of each rainbow, so each hard battle that you have you can always expect even the smallest amount of happiness that will amount to the biggest amount of happiness at the end of the war that you're fighting.

There are really good outlets out there even though it's so much easier to just fall back on the negative outlets because we have more in common with them during that phase in our life, or at least it's extremely easy to think that way. She herself though always had a connection to music, all kinds of music she could relate to in some way and some music was her party music that just made her happy just because. She could always depend on music, when she was little, music was just a really fun thing to listen to and of course it would cheer her up when she had a hard day, she loved singing and dancing without a care in the world, she didn't need it in the way that she needed it later on. When she turned 13 she started connecting to music from a really honest standpoint, music felt like a God-given gift to her, music pulled her back from jumping off the ledge when she was just fed up with it all, she could always count on music when she couldn't count on anyone else to be there. Just because someone is there for you, that doesn't mean that that alone makes them a true friend, having a true friend depends on if that person lifts you up or brings you down, even if you feel like you don't deserve to be happy which is never the case, everyone deserves to be able to trust someone no matter who needs it. Everyone deserves second chances, she mean life is too short to be angry or not let in the people who open heartedly admitted that they made mistakes, if they're too stubborn to admit that they aren't perfect then she understand, you don't really need someone in your life who can't fess up the truth when they know that they should, even if they know in their hearts that they were wrong but they just will not apologize with actual words, even if they just buy extravagant things for you. When everyone who swore that they would be there for her when she needed them and they bailed because they just said it to seem like they were real friends because they knew that she was always there, music was her true friend that dried her tears when she cried, music was her friend, her family, her rescue, her partner in crime, music was always down for whatever, music didn't leave her when everyone else did. She fell back on the words that the songs said, how the beat made her feel, she paid the most attention to the message of the song, she closed her eyes so that she could really connect to the lyrics and it took her to her safe place at the same time, it was like no one could hurt her when music spoke to her, she knew she could escape and it was better than any plane ticket that money could buy her. She appreciated piano ballads the most because you could hear the pain or the truth that was telling the story. She always imagined herself on stage singing like the messages she heard in front of so many people and that thought especially helped her when she got to age 15 and she was going through a bunch of dark caves without a flashlight, she could always see that dream, she knew that if she saw millions of people and heard them screaming her name that she would understand that she went through what she went through for a reason.

An outlet she didn't use too much was a diary or a journal, when she had really bad days she would, it was helpful because she could vent without being judged, she couldn't do that with friends. She did have true friends but she had these voices in her head telling her that she was a burden and if she told her friends then they wouldn't really have time for it but they would pretend to care because "That's what friends do." The thing is though that's not what friends do, friends are there for you but her mind was her worst enemy so it diluted her into thinking that she was a burden and that she should go through her problems alone. Sure there were some things that she needed a psychiatrist for a lot of her problems, it just would've been cool to have a friend who didn't just ask her "How are you?" and just expecting her to say good instead of how she'd really doing. She only trusted herself and Psychiatrists though because it was just easier to trust her because she wouldn't run away, she couldn't run from herself not forever anyway, but Psychiatrists costed money so she was good venting on her own for a little while. She found her voice in poetry though, she could say whatever she wanted but it had to make sure that it rhymed which was a more creative outlet kind of like music, she was a colorful personality so she enjoyed writing poems. Writing poems and music were a little different from each other because she could hear the emotions in the story that the singer was singing or hear it in the melody, in poetry you could feel the words and what they were saying and feeling, so even though they were a little bit different from each other they still made her feel as equally free. She felt free because no one was judging her, she didn't really get to know that feeling as much as she could've, and she was always able to just didn't know that she could felt like it was inevitable for people to judge her for the way she walked and talked and thought, but she didn't know that it couldn't affect her if she just didn't care about what they said. It was really hard to just ignore the ignorance at first and it still is, especially because it happened every single step she took every single second of every single day and it wasn't the same person saying it.

She always felt like she needed to answer and tell them she was okay, and to other people that seemed like the polite thing for her to do but they walked perfectly so they didn't have to worry about them appearing to be drunk, but if she growing tired of talking back was rude then she wasn't going to be nice anymore. It annoyed her that they couldn't seem to give her a break, it made her sad and angry because it didn't really seem to matter how hard she was working to try and walk

"Normally," everyone could just see that she was different, but to them it was a "Dangerous" type of different because she looked as if she was going to fall down, but half the time she didn't fall especially once she was out of High School. She just had so many questions as to why she couldn't stop hearing those voices everywhere she went, and she was stuck on the thought that having Ataxia took away a part of her potential as if everything that she always wanted for her life required nothing being different about her, the whole diagnosis of Ataxia just really messed with her at that time, especially because apparently because Ataxia was more commonly found in people of European descent. The statistics of it isn't what truly bothered her, statistics had a part to play in it but mostly what bugged her about it was judgements, but the wisest advice about her Ataxia that she received was from her High School biology teacher and that advice was that just because she had all the things that came with Ataxia that didn't mean that her brain wasn't capable of everything that the brains of people who considered themselves "normal." She gave her what was probably the most helpful and encouraging advice that she ever had when it came to Ataxia, for some reason she always felt like just because it raised so much frustration for her that it messed with her mind, which was true, but little did she know that just because the judgements got to her head, that didn't mean that her brain was affected by what she was always told, it sounds so weird she know, but it felt to her like maybe there was a barrier or something between her brain and her mind, she felt like her mind was where she stored all her thoughts and some of those thoughts were meant to bring her down, but her brain helped her think of different ways to prove those thoughts wrong, it might sound weird but it made sense to her that her mind could be her worst enemy but her brain and her mind seemed to balance each other out pretty well, kind of like her brain and her mind were her two best friends. I guess because best friends challenge you when they know you can do it, but she never really looked at the positive side of her life besides Ataxia because she only focused on what she had heard and how if she took one step that was different than other people then apparently she was too different, but she didn't see that besides her balance, everyone else wasn't really all that different. The problem was that she was just looking at the big picture which was really hard to ignore, it was just so obvious for everyone to see that her balance was off, that was like a first impression for her because it was just the first thing people (including her) saw. She didn't see that that was just a tiny part of her story and if people wanted to focus on that as them already knowing enough about her before they even asked for her name well then they could think of her as a drunk or as a poor little sick girl or as whatever she looked like to them, if that's what they thought of me then they couldn't help themselves from thinking that because that's the first thing they saw, they could only help themselves from saying something rude out loud like calling her a drunk or something, but she could still control what she thought and what she knew about herself. She found out that they could judge all they wanted, but at the end of the day they weren't the ones who were there for her and they weren't the ones who she had to prove anything to, she knew that she was working as hard as she could to walk as best as she possibly could, and there were people worse off than her who weren't the least bit insecure about how they appeared, that didn't mean that she was selfish or ungrateful for being insecure about her situation, that just meant that she didn't have to worry about how she looked on the outside because she was just fine on the inside, that's just not something everyone can see right away and that was okay with her. When her teacher told her that though that's the first time she started to use a different perspective on what it meant, so that kind of made her start thinking the way she does today, because after that thought processed into her mind she started thinking realistically of all the businesses and other careers she could go into, and wouldn't it be ironically funny if all the enemies she had in the past decided to ask her for a job after she proved them wrong. It's supposed to irritate you when people ask you if you're okay every second, but she let the criticism motivate her, not everyone thought that it was criticism but she didn't see it as something else until she turned 21. So she didn't need to drink anymore, she didn't need to stuff her face with food because she was angry or sad because she couldn't do everything other people could do because she didn't walk as straight as they did, but there was a lot of things she could do even with her balance. It wasn't like she was diagnosed and couldn't do anything about it, for some reason when she heard the details of Ataxia she kind of looked at it like a death sentence because she felt like it stayed written clearly on her and there was no hiding it, but once she got the dark cloud out of her head, she realized that she could go back to Physical therapy to work on her balance, she could go to the gym because she didn't have to feel insecure and she didn't really want to stick with the dark cloud anymore. There was just something about chopping off her hair and losing all the weight and also having a plan to move out on her own that just made her feel like she was working on a new version of herself, and maybe she was finding who she used to be before she lost who she was, either way she was going to be the new version of herself that she was always missing, you just don't always know that you're missing something until you let that something go. She always just thought of pleasing everyone too much that she never really stopped trying to be perfect enough to ask herself if she was happy enough, all she was concerned about was how she looked to everyone else, but she couldn't see that there was no reason for her to care about their criticism because they weren't there at the end of the day. She didn't understand that part back then because she was too busy thinking about what she could do to win over the approval of people who were determined to not see her win, she didn't understand that she couldn't always win and even if she always did win, well then she wouldn't really ever be surprised that she won, that wouldn't really be any fun in her book. I think the best lesson in life comes to you after you fall because everytime you fall from that time on you run a little more before you hit the ground than you did the last time you fell, it's a positive thing to fall because that just means you're getting close to your destination. Life has this funny process of getting everyone to their own destiny by throwing them obstacles so they can understand how much work it takes to get there, but those obstacles are put there to keep us determined and our tears are there to remind us what we are fighting for. I'm going to tell you how I see it, the first obstacle is going to be a speed bump, it might be big it might be small, and that seed bump is on a road that leads you to a forest, the forest is there because it has a lot of rain and you'll see snakes and reptiles on one side and on the other side you'll see koalas and other cuddly and loving animals, the snakes are only going to make you cry but I'm not going to tell you to stay away from them, not all snakes are venomous, I'm just not a reptile loving person they're a little to slimy for my taste that's all, just make sure you stay away from the venomous ones, don't worry it'll be clear which ones have venom when you see them. I would be friend the other half of the forest with the Koalas and the other warm hearted responsible helpful animals, their responsible because they taught themselves to be, the snakes aren't venomous to everyone but sometimes they're just venous to you not always because they want to be but just because they aren't prepared to be in the next chapter of your life, but the Koala's are still there.

After you learn for the first time who the snakes in that part of your life are, that's when you leave the forest and then it gets easier in the next round because the exit out of the forest is the starting line of the jungle, there are going to be lions and Gorillas and Gazelles and the rest of the domestic animals out there and you're going to be scared at first, but the lion isn't there to hurt you but it is indeed there to roar. The Lion's roaring because it's roar is so loud that everyone can hear it and your voice is just as loud, in fact that lion roars so loud that it could make a difference in someone's life or in several people's lives, and that exactly everything that your voice is capable of doing and more, but you only get to the Roar once you stop being so scared and let people hear your roar. The gorilla is the fiercest and strongest animal in the jungle known for its strength and everyone respects its dominance and listens to what the gorilla says because everyone knows that the Gorilla is wise and knows what they're doing, when it comes to you it means you're wise and responsible enough for people to not correct you every second and they can let you go a little bit each time you do what you meant to do. The Gazelle is really fast and it has a generous and good heart, it's caring, gentle, peaceful, wise, kind and considerate but knows when to swallow their pride and when to stand up and say something's not right, but it does know how to fight so don't mess with the Gazelle.

With all those animals you get to start getting to know who you are, those are all the qualities that you need for every path you take in your life, and when you find who you are you'll know, and then you'll find your way out of the jungle and at the start of the climb onto Mt. Fiji, one of the world's tallest mountains, the mountain is only as tall as you make it, and it depends on how much you got past in the jungle and in the forest and the size of your dream is one of the key elements that decide the height of the mountain that you get to climb to finish your next chapter. It takes a lot of preparation and a whole lot of guts plus a lengthy amount of time and of course planning ahead, Mount

Fiji is a mountain that some people can't even survive climbing on, because your Mount Fiji is made to fit your destiny and not anyone else's, everyone has their own Mount Fiji and the more that they can handle means that the mountain will be that much taller and it'll take that much longer to climb to the top. Some people won't make it to the top but that's just because that climb isn't their journey to take, but you don't have to be scared of your own destiny they only took another route so you could finish your climb alone because finding yourself is something only you can do, some journeys are just for you alone and that doesn't mean you won't have friends climb the mountain with you, friends can climb the mountain with you but once you reach the top you're all standing on top of your own mountains because you're all on your own mountains after everyone else leaves to take another route. You're never given a taller mountain than you can handle climbing up, You're life is designed to be your climb and your climb is a masterpiece that isn't finished until your climb is finished, and don't be afraid to fall because if you didn't then you wouldn't be climbing the right climb, You falling doesn't mean you fell off the mountain that just means you fell down because you were too close to the top and there's always someone who doesn't want you to get to the top, but way more people who do want you to reach the top. No matter how many times you fall down, you're prone to get back up but the only thing is that you decide when you get up and you also decide if you want to get back up or if you just sit back and watch life pass you by, and the other thing is that once you decide to sit back and let life pass you by, then it becomes absolutely impossible for you to be able to jump back in once you do take that seat, it doesn't even matter how big of a Game changer opportunity is so close to you that you can almost touch it, that keyword will always be "Almost" because you chose to give up. Now I'm not saying that to be harsh, I'm saying that you had a choice because even though it was almost impossible to see that you had a choice, you always had the control over yourself but you didn't see that you had it because you wanted to believe that they were right, but they weren't. Just because they were right at one point in time or even if they were right so many times in the past or even for your whole life or most of it, just because they've led you in the right direction before don't let them mislead you because you trusted them so much, because your heart will feel damage that you didn't feel back when they were right.

CHAPTER 4
THE LION

You have your own voice even when you can't see it, sometimes you go with people who have our trust when we can't see how they abused it. We let that trust blind us and lead us to go down their path and forget about our own, so now your name doesn't even belong to you because you're not being who you are. I know it can be so hard and it might feel like you can't take one more step further by yourself, but you have to honestly know that when everyone else is gone you can always depend on you, and that's how you'll learn to speak your mind, even though we love and trust people that doesn't mean that you're not going to have a difference of opinion with that person. Sometimes we forgot that we had our own voice before we trusted that person and it's not bad that you trust and love so deeply, but you can never lose the person you are, whether it's a friend who was never wrong before or someone that you strongly believed would never turn on you no matter what you still know what you believe and what is right, if you don't speak up you might regret it and life is too short for regrets because you never know what's coming tomorrow. We are not people that can ever be defined, unless you walked a mile in someone else's shoes then you don't know what that person is going through, and disguises can easily fool you, they can fool anyone so never assume.

Don't ever let a smile fool you, a smile does mean you're kind but it doesn't mean you're weak, you don't have to avoid conflict to be strong and you don't need to keep quiet because you're scared to hear what someone else says because even though life is too short to have regrets life is also too short to hold back what you feel.

A lion is feared by all of the animals of the jungle because they're the fiercest animals in the jungle and their roar is what earns them respect because it shows that they fear nothing, some lions eat the Gazelle because they decide that they want an early lunch, but some lions are trained. Now just because the Lions are trained that doesn't mean that they have to be caged or tamed, that just means that those Lions are have no reason to hurt you, just because you're fierce does not make you a monster, it means you won't let anyone trample over you, you can be fierce and have a voice.

Being fierce means that you earned respect and everyone knows not to take advantage of you, fierceness doesn't make you an ugly person and it doesn't make you unreasonable, stubbornness and fierceness are two very different things. Being Stubborn means you can't swallow your pride and admit that you're wrong, no matter how wrong someone is they just can't put aside their pride for just one measly minute and Stubbornness in the wrong way is not a very pretty quality, even Lions should admit that they're wrong when they're wrong, especially when they're right a lot of the time. Admitting your wrong proves that you're strong and mature enough to admit what a lot of other people can't do, not many people can say that they're wrong they can only think it and sometimes they can't even face that in their own head, but it takes someone with a really true heart to be true to themselves. If you can't face that you're wrong even in your own mind then you aren't being true to who you are, apologize when you could've handled a situation better don't let your pride get in the way, because there's no more asking "What if?" anymore because you can't go back and change it because that moment is coming back. Time machines don't exist and moments only come once, there can be a moment that is extremely similar to another moment, but that's only the image of the same moment not the same moment itself but rather it's just a copy of the moment, so treasure moments because a moment is once but life is long enough, moments pass, don't let it pass you up.

Lions cry, that doesn't make them weak, allowing their tears to fall makes them smart because they know how unhealthy it is to hold their tears inside and they are brave for not being afraid of hearing what other people are going to say about it, because Lions know that someone is going to say something. I have another animal metaphor for you guys and it might sound funny the way I worded it, but here it goes, the Gorilla might laugh at lion when the Lion's cries, but the Lion won't laugh when the Gorilla cries because part of being a Lion is understanding Forgiveness is the key to stop crying over what isn't going to change, the Gorilla won't laugh at the lion again because the Lion wasn't hurt by the Gorilla. If the lion was hurt then the Lion would have fought hate with more hatred but the Lion is showing that love makes him stronger so much that the Gorilla looks to the lion when in a rut, the Lion is the bigger person while the Gorilla is learning, you need the heart of a lion to have the heart of a warrior.

Another part of being a Lion is taking responsibility, if something is wrong then don't do it and ask for Forgiveness later when you knew you shouldn't have done it, just explain why you're going to do it and the only way you can know if it's the right thing to do is if you take a second to just honestly ask yourself if it's the right or wrong thing or right thing for you. No one knows you better than you, so you are the only one who knows what is for you, people might think they know what's best for you but they need to accept the fact that you are you first therefore deep down inside you know what suits you.

Lions only use their claws when they need to open a can or something, not for fighting physically Lions aren't afraid to use their roar for that, using their claws doesn't solve anything, using their roar gets them what they need and their gets them where they need to be. Claws are used if the Lion is attacked, but never if the Lion is not bothered by another claw, despite what people say about Lions they're actually really peaceful animals until of course they are hurt, there are several ways that the Lion can be hurt, if you mess with the Lions loved ones then you mess with the lion then you should be afraid of their roar but be afraid of hurting them because a lion's heart turned to stone is no longer a Lion. Lions don't keep stone cold hearts in them, Lions let it go even when it's so hard to do because Lions never let themselves wallow or dwell on the past because when they have nothing weighing on them they are unstoppable and no matter who you are you can't get in their way if they forgive you. Forgiveness is probably the best quality that a Lion keeps besides Independence, they provide for themselves and for their cubs, and for everything that is right stand up, Lions think for themselves and help everyone else, because if The lion finds a dollar then someone they help gets 50 cents.

Now Gorillas have a lot of the same qualities as Lions especially when it comes to providing, Gorillas are just a tad bit different than Lions though. Gorillas are not known for fierceness the most like Lions are, but instead Gorillas are known more for their physical strength and they shoe it by banging their chest to the East and the west, and the way they do that shows how confident they are. Because the Gorilla bangs on his chest does not mean that you need to physically bang on your chest just to be strong and have confidence, that just means that emotionally you gain confidence by having Respect, forgiveness, responsibility for your actions, and independence. These qualities are exactly what makes the Lion and the Gorilla very widely known as the strongest and fiercest animals of the jungle, now just because you have the heart of a Lion or a Gorilla or both doesn't mean that you're an animal it just means that no one smart will mess with you because of how you present yourself. And let's not forget how smart both of these Animals are, they can be sneaky but not in a bad way just in a "Teenage time to rebel "kind of way, which is a phase we all have gone through in our past no matter what we would like to describe phase as, but if you look at Domestic animals from an honest viewpoint then you'll see that they only have a few characteristics that differ from Humans, but they are more alike to humans than we thought.

Enough with Lions though I think you get the point already, a similar figure is something or Someone who is not afraid of anything, I don't mean little things like spiders, I think a lot of us don't like spiders, but that's not what I'm talking about, sorry guys I get off topic a lot. A warrior can be anyone, for me the way I see it, Life is a battle and we build armor around our heats to protect us from our enemies, sometimes our only enemy is the world. Our shields are up so that the enemy can get close to our hearts that are guarded, so there's no chance that they can get to our hearts, not even close and our swords are there to fight back against the enemy but it hasn't been touched so it has rusted because you've been too afraid to face your enemy. Your words are enough to cut through like sword without physically hurting the enemy, your armor is as thick as the tears you've cried, your shield is as big as the anger, frustration and hurt you've built up over the years and your shield is what the enemy used to laugh at, but the enemy isn't laughing anymore because now your enemy has led you to go to war, they never intended never thought you would fight back, you've taken over the battle that you've lost but now you'll win the war.

You can lose a whole lot of battles but that doesn't mean that you won't win the war, all those battles were tests that led to the war, tests that were designed to lead you far enough to the war. The tests are specially designed to have enough obstacles for you to go through until you get to the war, but if you're not there anymore then that race/obstacle course was set up for nothing, wasn't it? Even when it seems impossible, with every move that you make after that thought appears in your mind, it starts to get less and less impossible with every further step you take, it might feel like you can't do it anymore, but you just gotta give it a little time until you can think clearly because in that single moment you can't see anything but the pain and you only think if erasing it completely. Although Later on down the line you'll regret it and you'll figure out that the pain is still there but now it's just more permanent because you jumped off the ledge but you can't climb back on anymore, that's not how it works. Once you have armor on you just can't simply take it off, the thickness of it can wear off once you let your guard down, once you learn that not every situation is going to be like the last one you came out of, it takes a while to totally accept that what happened then isn't "supposed" to happen to you the way it did. Now when I say it wasn't supposed to happen to us I mean that we might feel like that was payback or the universe telling us that we just didn't deserve good things like we wished, but that moment that helped create your armor didn't happen to you because you deserved it, but that moment happened because your heart knew it's limits and knew that you would come out of every future situation ten times stronger/ just because you feel like the water is getting to steep and the tides are making it hard to breathe, your heart is the one breathing for you and life has a funny process of working things out, so funny that your heart is not created with the sense of misleading you therefore your heart doesn't have the ability to lead you into situations that you just can't emotionally take, sometimes we get our mind and our heart confused. Our mind and our heart both say different things, your mind and your heart usually are on opposite sides with each other, your mind wants to challenge you and your mind also hears comments that get negativity stuck in there and that negativity works with the challenging tasks that your mind throws at you, but your heart is realistic and knows exactly what you can handle, it's almost like your mind runs the challenging task at your to get your heart's ok and it's up to your heart to give your mind the "okay" to give you that challenging task. Your mind may be new to the party and just learning how to function in rhythm with you, but your heart knows you better then you know you, your heart will get you in and out of a lot of wars in life but as always your heart knows exactly when to pull you out, so when you feel like you are drowning just give it time to lay out a path for you. Just like a warrior, you have no idea what the next battle is going to bring you, but that doesn't mean because you're so scared of what the battle will do to you that you back out of the war entirely, and to finish the war you need to get through each battle first. If you don't finish every battle that you come upon but you still expect to take credit for winning the war, that's kind of like someone looking over all your test answers and claiming that they had no help with passing the class after they ace the midterm but with YOUR knowledge instead of their own.

I'm not going to try to say that I've been there or that I know what you are going through but I can say that I have an idea of how you are feeling, you are not weak because you don't think that you can go any further, you aren't selfish because you don't want the same old pain that you've been stuck with for a while, you're not being careless because so many people love you but you're still in pain, yeah you shouldn't hurt yourself because that's going to hurt them, but don't apologize for feeling the way you do, don't hide your tears because you think people won't look up to you if you let the tears fall down. Warriors don't apologize before every battle simply because they have to fight it, it's not the job of a warrior to fight from within it is a Warrior's destiny to fight with everything they have in them and to get their everything back paid to them in interest.

What I mean when I say interest is that when a warrior gives everything they have from deep inside them,(not internal organs or anything of that sort), then those warriors only end up being able to overcome way more than they ever could have expected, and those dark moments and days and months and years that they used to have in the past, those moments can only be seen in the light because all those moments got them to the point where they can barely look out into the world and see any limitations to what they can achieve.

Even a warrior needs to take time to heal from their battle wounds, there's no Gorilla out there who can ignore when everything falls down around them, there's no Lion that can be found within miles of here who doesn't get tired of roaring because it feels like no one's listening, but if it roars loud enough then people will hear it, if the Gorilla beats on its chest to make its statement clear then people will listen to what the Gorilla is saying, and when a warrior comes out of a battle with scratches on his/her body but is still standing strong then the crowds watching start to cheer. So when you're feeling weak remember that everyone has those moments that almost eat them alive, and when you're feeling like you don't know what to do just know that someone else is saying that same thing about themselves, and when you're saying that you wish that you weren't going through what you are going through at that moment then someone is saying how they wish that you weren't going through it either, but the most important thing for you to know is that you have someone who needs you here and supports you and wants you to have what you want for you and you only, meaning that that person is truly there for you and you can trust them, always. If that person is there for you then make sure that you are truly there for them, because if that's your true friend then you can be sure that you can trust them always, and true friends don't look at hearing you out as a job, true friends stick with you until the end because they want to be there, not because they have to. If they had to be there then that wouldn't really be a friendship, that would be a job as a servant or a maid, but we don't deserve to have "friends" who stand by you only because of your money, you deserve true friends and nothing else, so if you want a true friend then you gotta make sure that you yourself are a true friend first, because at the end of the day you gotta just ask yourself who's there for you when you need them to be. Don't worry, it'll come naturally to you, once you honestly trust someone you just get the feeling that when they crash down you'll be there to make sure they're landing is safe, truth is our comfort ones, lies make us uneasy even if we don't want to admit it, no one is born into this world with bad intentions that's just not the way this world works. Sometimes we just get too caught up in caring about the world's opinion of us that we are misled to the path of negative ethics, but we are not bad influences, we are all individuals so we all know right from wrong at the end of the day, now if we always do what's right is a different story. At certain times depending on the situation, it can sometimes be really hard to do what's right, that doesn't mean that that excuses for why we did the wrong thing but it just shows that doing the right thing isn't always easy, but I'm not going to tell you to tread on eggshells trying to do what is right every second because the "Perfect" life is pretty boring and lonely if you ask me, your life may not be absolutely perfect but it is your "Perfect "and that's all anyone can ask for.

CHAPTER 5
STORIES

She looked in the mirror so many times and hated everything that she saw, and she didn't try everything to not feel that way either because she felt like she deserved to be at the point in her life where she felt that bad about herself. She couldn't see past the tears that dropped from her eyes, she couldn't see that the pain was leading her to do ugly things but instead she only saw that she had ugliness on her, pain misleads people to do whatever they can to feel better, it's not easy for them to see who they really are and they can't see their true beauty when they can only see darkness without the flashlight that is and always was their own.

She tried to put on make-up and she tried to lose weight and look like she wasn't who she was on the inside, but she couldn't see the big picture, which was that she wasn't ugly but what she was doing to herself was the only thing that that was ugly in that situation. She couldn't see that changing herself was what wasn't a pretty sight, she never had to be a model or a Barbie doll to be beautiful, and it sounds so cheesy too say that Beauty comes from the inside and not out so I won't tell you that, what I will tell you is that Beauty starts on the inside and it shines through the outside, so no make-up or masks needed, beauty is what you make it just like life is the amount of beauty that you make it, there's a major difference between pretty and beautiful, it might take work to get pretty every single day but we're all born with Beauty, it's up to you to grow that beauty instead of hiding it by moving too fast because other people try to define what you should look like, because when people try to define you and show you what they think you should be, the image that they showed you usually isn't even a good enough image for them to live out. Every word that she heard from them always stuck with her because she lived for everyone else's approval but didn't once pay attention to what she approved of because she wasn't trying to impress herself, she was erasing who she was because she wanted to impress her enemies when she already did impress them but she just couldn't tell that she did because instead of reading between the lines to look through to the truth, she just believed all that society told her and took them for their word.

Everyone always told her what's on the inside that makes you beautiful and not what's on the outside, but she could never bring herself to honestly believe that, it kind of is extremely corny to hear now though because it's been said so many times before, so I can't tell you that that is an entirely true statement, but what I will tell you is that this statement is partly true but not the whole story. The whole story is that the beauty that you've always had inside of you from day 1 shines through to the outside, beauty is being a good person, beauty isn't finding foundation that won't damage your skin, make-up is a powder to make your face look a bit or even a lot different than you usually look, but make-up fades away as you cry but your face always stays with you until the end. I'm not saying Make-up is bad all I'm saying is that Pretty and different are two different things, I'm not saying you have to choose between the two either because you can be pretty on top of the beauty that you have and have always had, I am saying that you don't need a different look on your face in order to be beautiful because you already are, sometimes we just need a magnifying glass to tell us that the beauty's always been there.

The last time that she could have recalled that she was skinny was back when she was 12 years old, she just turned 21 years old and she was far from that shape, which made total sense that she changed from what size she was from 9 years ago, but she wasn't fit for her age or even close because of her binge eating. She binge ate because every time she hit the gym with intentions of losing weight, she always seemed to give up once she saw how hard it was to lose the least amount of weight, it was just hard for her to stay motivated when her mind told her that she was making up everything, including making up her own pain. It makes no sense to me that anyone would actually make pain for themselves if they didn't have any pain in them to begin with, she use to get furious when people claimed that she acted the way she did for attention, as if she cried until she got a thousand headaches over and over just for attention and it drove me crazy for a while, that is of course until she cared about what she thought instead of what they thought. The moment when she realized that she didn't need to impress at all was probably when she discovered the next chapter of who she was, it took a lot of work to block out all the negativity, but it took having life lessons of keeping fake friends, a whole lot of setbacks that she thought were failures, a whole lot of heartbreak and a blurry perception of who she was in order to come to a point in her life where she was halfway okay. She was okay with -being halfway okay because in order for anyone to be happy they have to be okay, and halfway was almost there, she was content with being that "half okay" girl for a while, especially because she wasn't crying until she got a headache every single day.

Another story I'll tell you is when she went to Africa to see one of her friends who was sick at the time and when they would go out places everyone would just stare at her because she was sick, she could remember a time that she felt like yelling out to everyone looking at her to stop staring at her as if they haven't ever seen someone who wasn't perfect before. "What is wrong with you people? There's nothing to see here, stop staring and go back to eating your food for Goodness sakes," is what she wanted to yell out at everyone who was staring at that moment, they were all at a restaurant celebrating my birthday, something she hadn't done since she was 12 years old, it just made her so angry that she had to not only worry about her own illness, but on top of that she felt like she had to worry about what the rest of the world had to say about her, even if they didn't mean to be rude by staring it still ticked her off. It angered her because people with disabilities do everything that they possibly can to not feel diabled and to not look disabled to the rest of the world, people who are disabled no matter how big or small the disability work twice as hard as everyone else who seems to be "normal" just so there's a possibility that no one will say anything, it just takes while to realize that you have to learn to not care about what other people say. This world isn't going to change overnight, but we can change how we view the criticism that the world throws at us whenever we want, because the world controls their words and their actions, but they can't control you and if you break down from their criticism so the bottom line is that if you want to change the world you have to start with you, because they might say that they're going to change but actions speak louder than words, and you don't know if they're going to let you down but you can only be sure of if you'll be there, and it's the best feeling ever, just knowing that you can know for sure that someone will always be there. So at the end of the day it doesn't even matter what they say because they haven't seen that girl going to physical therapy, or that boy who walks so well that he doesn't need to use a walker anymore, so ignore the hate and just focus and you because you might not walk as Perfect as everyone else but you can run to your dream just as well as they can and sometimes even faster.

While she was in Africa, she experimented and tried to stop eating, she was there for almost two months so she figured that that was enough time to just focus on losing weight. When she did that she felt light-headed when she stood up and that made her feel happy because with that and the headache she had it was beginning to feel like she was too weak to think or do anything that might've made her feel bad, the only thing that distracted her from wanting to eat even one small French fry was her remembering the image of herself in her head that she wanted to look like, but her starving herself didn't do her any good, she tried to same thing before while she was in the U.S., but it never worked out, and it wasn't working then either. When she had a goal in her mind she just had to stick with it, even if her attempts of achieving that goal through the way that she wanted to achieve it failed, she still was just too stubborn to try it another way because her mind was already set on going by that routine. The truth was losing weight that way was dangerous and the odds were it would never work by the way that she intended it to, because it's possible to be physically fit and look healthy on the outside, but you can still be extremely unhealthy on the outside, and the health issues that you have in the end when you look the way you want to look aren't even worth it anymore to be completely honest. Sometimes we all just do whatever we can to fit the mold that society had sculpted for them to fit into, so much that we just totally change to a whole new person because Society said that you were too "boring" or too "different", but they forgot to tell you the truth, that we're not all supposed to be normal, that being different is unique and a 1 in a million quality. Changing who you are makes you weak because you're surrendering to society's wants but their wants are not a need, there's a difference between what people want and what they need, someone who doesn't know you doesn't have a need for you to fit the mold that they sculpted, they just want to be someone who can take credit for changing you into the image that society thinks is the image of success. Although what some people don't understand is that you cannot judge a book by its cover because every time you do judge a book by its cover, the rest of the book is way more complex story than what you saw on the cover, so always make sure to read the whole book before jumping to conclusions.

She took another trip while she was in Africa and she hiked up a mountain that led to a 7-day retreat to a monastery, she went with her Mom, her Aunt, her cousins, her sister and her Uncle, however, her stay wasn't very pleasant. The path to the monastery was extremely rocky and everyone, even people who didn't have a balance problem, still had some trouble walking up the path, it took her two hours or more to hike up that hill and it was kind of a hike of emotions as well, she kept getting so mad at herself for every wrong step that she would take as if she was "supposed" to be walking perfectly on a path of uneven rocks, no one else was but she felt like she should walk like she had no differences inside of her because once someone starts to work twice as hard to be able to keep up it just kind of comes naturally to them after a while and they don't feel like they should take a break from trying too hard. After a long two hours of hiking, she reached the top along with her Uncle and Sister where she saw her family waiting for her thinking that something happened too them because they all knew that there were a few issues involved with me hiking up a hill with her Uncle and sister, and the funny thing is that she was the first one who they were so surprised to see. It was scary for any foreigner to hike up that hill as rocky and as long a walk as it was, it made her feel insecure that no matter how hard she tried to do good she could never hide the fact that she had a balance problem, but to her she did feel like a lot of people worried because they cared, but on the other hand she also understood that she had that balance problem for as long as she could remember, therefore, even though they cared that didn't mean that they had to keep asking if she was ok after they had already heard the answer that she gave to that question a hundred times over. She was grateful that she had so many people who cared, but at the same time she just wished that everyone would just give her a break and accept that she was okay despite the fact that she didn't walk or run or jump perfectly, it got really tiring trying to please everyone when it was impossible to please them in the first place. When she got to the top of the hill her Mom, her Aunt and her Grandma were all crying because they thought that something bad happened to her, her Mom actually said to her Grandma that she thought that she killed her daughter by bringing her to that hike, but that was a little bit too germatic as far as she was concerned and so they all sat there together as if everything was just fine. It wasn't fine, it was like she was a doll who had the whole world watching her every single step so that they could pity her every time she fell down, but it's not like she wanted to fall down, but when she did happen to fall down she wanted to fall down like she didn't care who was watching, and eventually she did because if she always told whoever was watching that she was okay every 5 seconds, which is the time length that it seemed to take before she stumbled on a step, but if that was the case then she would have never gotten up because it wouldn't have made a difference in what they would think. She got back up knowing that her getting up would not get them to change their assumptions nor would it get them to stop voices their not-so-positive opinions, she could stay up all night and all day but all still would not make any difference at all, so she eventually accepted that she couldn't win, and after a few months of learning how to face that head on then she learned that she could really be okay even with the judgements.

So while she was up there, there was a daily routine that she needed to follow that consisted of her hiking down the path that was part of the monastery and full of more rocks both big and small, and that path would lead her to a path that was way more uneven and when she got to her destination she was supposed to bathe herself in holy water, she didn't mind drinking holy water but instead it was the way that people described why they thought she needed it. A lot of people that she knew of in that culture got the impression that she walked like she did because she was possessed or something, and the holy water was supposed to make her walk perfectly, I believe that Holy water can do a lot of Good things but She knew that God gave her that fight for a reason and she didn't have it because she did something wrong, she was given that fight because God knew that she could handle it and that it would only make her stronger, but apparently she wasn't diagnosed with it instead she was punished with it, if you asked her family of course.

She was expected to go through that routine for seven days straight but she ended up going through that routine for four days, besides the fact that the living environment was just so different from the U.S and took some time for her to adjust to, she was just hurt that they all saw her as if she did that to herself, out of everything that had happened to her she was hurt the most just knowing that the people who were supposedly close to her thought those things about her.

It was day number four that she walked down that path to receive the holy water that everyone was pushing her to go get, and it was the worst day that she had out of the days that she had there because she was in Physical pain, she had been sleeping on a mattress on the rocky hard cement floor for pretty much every night that she was there, not to mention she fell on a bunch of rocks and landed on her back earlier that day, so it was understandable that her back was hurting as much as it was. It felt like a bowling literally had landed on her back as if her back looked like a bunch of bowling pins and someone bowled a strike, she was told by someone that she could just head back up the path instead of going forward like she had the past two days, but she was just the type of person who always needed to prove people wrong no matter what, therefore she refused to go back, but when she got to the bottom of the path she had no idea how she would get back to the top of the path. Once she started back up the path, her back hurt so much that she could barely take one step forward without crying, it probably took her about 30 minutes to an hour to get back to the top of the path, she just felt like that was her breaking point and she just felt like staying on that path by herself so she could just stop the pain for a minute, for once in her life she knew how to stop the pain. She didn't stop though she took a couple of breaks which was only forcing her to endure the pain she was feeling a bit longer, but once she got to the top she thought things couldn't get worse but boy was she wrong, Her Aunt asked what was wrong and the girl's Mom told her about how bad her back was hurting her and she said something that frustrated her even more. Her Aunt said that her feeling the pain that she was at the moment was the way that God was expressing that she would be healed soon, Healed from what? Was she really saying that God was punishing her just to heal her? Then she must've been in line to be healed for her whole life because she always had some kind of physical pain, especially when she slept on a stone hard floor for the past 3 nights, but no matter her Aunt's intentions that statement extremely angered her because in her eyes that was the furthest thing from the truth.

So after hearing all the judgements that she had always heard, she went back up the path to where her family was, she just laid there until they went back to the house they were staying at, and the people there at the monastery of course made it their mission to say how ungrateful and how bad of a person she was being for not going through the daily routine that the monastery had set, and of course they claimed that it was the demons inside of her not wanting her to go down to finish the seven days, but it's wasn't like she hadn't heard things like that said about her in the past, so she didn't let it bother her at all, she was just happy to get out of there and into a more comfortable place which she and her family stayed at while they were in Africa. When she got back it was little that she knew that the vacation she was on would be the major climax of her life, after all that she had gone through there was just something about going back home and being near family that showed her how to start putting the puzzle pieces back together, she had a lot of time to think which is something that she normally hated being able to do, but she hated thinking only because she would over-think and under think but never think to the point where it was just right, but this time was different because she wasn't trying to beat herself up no matter how stuck she was feeling and she wasn't letting the voices but in because she already knew their goal and she had heard their speech way too many times before, she was only listening to the girl who she hadn't heard from in a while, her own voice.

After she took a moment to herself about five and a half years later, while she was in Africa, she realized at that moment that she was too tired to waste all her energy just killing herself every day just to silence the demons inside her head who told her that she wasn't good enough. The demons in her head that led her to doubt herself for so long, but she finally had a moment of realization where she finally realized that the voices in her head were only messing with her to get her to the position that she was slowly deteriorating to by agreeing with the things that they said about her, those voices were using her to break herself down because that's what they wanted and what they strive to see, they work to see how badly they can break different people down.

She was proving them right, she was showing them that they won, but she was too filled with the hate that the voices let her see that she felt like she was fighting too hard and she thought she could just take a break and nothing would change, she thought that she could just ignore the voices for a while and that she could just basically pick up where she left off as if those voices wouldn't be talking about her behind her back while she was gone. The target that the voices were aiming at was getting to see how negatively their hate affected her, it was like a race for them, therefore, they didn't care how long she stepped back for because they would just keep talking negatively about her until they her heard a crackle or two in her which is how they knew that she was close to breaking. But then came a day that the voices dreaded to see, and that was the day that she decided to stop feeling sorry for herself because she knew that did nothing but give them energy, she was done rewarding the voices for trying to hurt her instead of punishing them for it. The best way that she could punish them was by trying to be happy, that didn't mean that she had to be happy right away, but every second that she wasn't crying was a second of silence where the voices were concerned, nothing could bring her down if she didn't let it, so from then on she wasn't concerned with the past and getting back that time that she gave to everything that wanted to see her fail, she was concerned about starting from scratch and becoming a different and a better person because she didn't have a time machine so she couldn't go back and change it, and even if she could she soon decided that she wouldn't change a thing about her past because all those things made her who she was and who she is today, so even though she'd done things in her past that she wasn't proud of, she would've been a different person if she'd done everything perfectly. She wasn't totally happy even at that point where she finally found out how to be okay, you see just because she found a way that she could be happy doesn't mean that it was currently happening, but that didn't mean that her days didn't get any brighter, if her days didn't get brighter then she would've been searching for that flashlight that she lost for a whole lot longer, but she found the flashlight and it was a little prolonged but well worth it even though that five and a half years was absolute hell to go through she still wouldn't have changed a thing about that whole experience because if she did then she would have to find who she was all over again, and again, and so on and so on, because when she was stuck in that dark cave that flashlight was the only thing that led her out and if she didn't get stuck in the cave then she wouldn't have needed the flashlight, what I mean is she didn't know that she was lost until she tried to find herself, it was kind of like there was a point years and years ago where she was convinced that she knew who she was as well as she could know herself, so she looked deep inside her soul and knocked on the door to find her heart, but she wasn't anywhere to be found.

She wasn't exactly jumping Sky-high out of her bed every morning as she woke up, but she was in a much better place than she was a couple of years ago, she had scars but not the kind that caused bruises, but the scars only reminded her of where she was, where she would never again go, and where she had to stop by to be who she is today. She was in the process of discovering new things and one of those things were new ways to express herself, she started an obsession with tattoos, but only tattoos that meant something to her, tattoos aren't for everyone though, some people take up art or music, cooking, which can be unhealthy at times, but as long as you eat to your limit you'll be okay. Music was still her muse but now she had two muses, Music and writing, writing and poetry was her way to vent so she would just keep a journal with a bonus because the journal had a picture of her favorite singer on the front cover, but the tattoos were more to remind her how far she had come, when she had to be reminded of that and the scars hurt too much to look at, it was just another one of those outlets, except it was a healthier one because she wasn't addicted to it, it was just poetry on her arm if you asked her, but to others it might have been a bit extreme of an outlet but then again not everyone has to understand the unique expressions that people give. She didn't have to be afraid of her thoughts anymore because when she would think, it wouldn't drive her crazy anymore but instead she thought 1 step ahead instead of thinking 5 steps back, She used to think of something and then have a million and one questions pop up in her head and the questions were "What if?," and "How come?," "Why not?" but the "What if?" is what almost always sent her to the breaking point. Now instead of thinking "What if I can't do it?" she started thinking things like "What happens after this plan of mine takes off?," she had that perspective because she looked at other people who were going through a rougher time and those people weren't as sad as she was because they already learned that complaining about what they didn't have wouldn't change what they actually did have and the time that they would have been taking to complain about that particular situation was time that they could have been using to figure out how they could be making the best out of what they had because it wasn't like there was a time machine that they could hop into to change the moment that started their current situation, so they figured that if everything that they could do in that moment could not change that specific thing that changed their life, they figured that out by thinking that if it was a biological disorder that was started on the inside of their body, then they couldn't do anything themselves to change that it was there, they could make it better though. To make it better all they'd have to do was look up at their options, for example, the girl that I told you about who had Ataxia went to physical therapy to work on being physically strong enough to walk as well as she possibly could, each situation has a solution and the solution does not need to be a cure to make sure that you are ok, the solution just needs to be one that gives you everything that you need to be who you are because it's all about Definition, like I said before, whatever qualities that are different about you are defined by you and not the other way around, so you make your qualities look and feel like you want them to make you look and feel.

So with that new method of thinking there was three people that she also needed to remember and take along on her journey with her, because you can say that these three people helped her become the woman who she is today, and she could always be %100 sure that all three people would be there with her no matter what she was going through and they never seemed to disappoint either. The first person was named "Me", and she was the one with all the funny qualities who always made her laugh and brought all the great qualities that a true friend with the most true intentions would bring into her life. The second person was named myself and myself was someone who gave her words of wisdom when she was hurt and confused and not to mention that myself was a "Ride or Die" type of friend, the type of friend that is so hard to find but once you find one you make sure to keep them. Last but not least, her third person to tag along on her journey until the end was named I, and I was the part of her that only she defined, I was who she was, "I" was independent and courageous, Her and "I" were inseparable and their thoughts were in sync with one another, and most importantly "I" reminded her who she was because "I" showed her own reflection. Me, myself and "I" along with the girl were an unstoppable trio, together they would all ride together in one car no matter the destination and no matter time, they passed each of the broke down roads to leave them in their past and they never looked back, they kept those experiences close to their hearts but that didn't in any way mean that they wanted to go back to the start, they were okay with the light that they had recently found and they could wait a while for a voltage upgrade. She was content on hanging out with her new friend "Me," her new friend who wasn't so new because "Me" was always with her but she couldn't tell until she really needed her, and "Myself" was a good friend who she lost contact with for a really long while but when she finally reached out to her it was like she forgot who she was for the longest time and didn't know until she saw "myself" looking back at her in the mirror.

Me" showed her the happy side, myself showed her the realistic side of everything, and "I" showed her all that she could make of that reality, so at the end of the day she found out that she had three Alter egos who turned out to be her truest friends who kept her grounded, who reminded her why she laughs, and who reminded her of who was always in the mirror. All three of them had a whole lot more to explore but if they got through that long five and a half years with each other then they could say for the first time in their lives that they could be confident in knowing they could get through anything else that the world had to throw at them and the only way they could do that was by leaning on each other.

Finally, the road that they had been driving on had come to an end and there were construction cones that read out to the them what other road they could take to get to their destination, because that road was already driven on too many times by each one of them but they kept making U-turns and detours in hopes that they would stumble upon a shortcut along the way, but it was about time for a new road with New stories and new adventures, so they all made one last detour which took them for a ride with new views, new feelings and much brighter days, and their mission from now on was to live life like tomorrow didn't exist. It's amazing how so many qualities can fit in one person, but everyone has their own "me, myself, and I, "and those sides of us are essential to us all living life the way we want to because they remind us of the kind of life that we really want and they also have a way of separating our fairytales and fantasies from reality. As they all watched so many of the roads that they've traveled through burn down as they crossed it, they ended that last chapter of their lives and finally started a new one, and to finish the last chapter and start on their new chapter all they had to do was put a tank of gas in their car just enough Gas to get them started onto the new road ahead of them, and once they had enough to start them on that road, they were pretty good at going with the flow, once they really wanted to get somewhere they would do whatever they had to do to get there. So once they put the gas in the car "Me" closed the tank, "Myself" started the ignition, and finally "I" put both hands on the wheel with her eyes up ahead on the road to see all that was ahead, never what was behind them though, they looked behind them way too many times before and now they were never tempted to look back either. Me, myself, and I always had each other to lean on but that didn't count until now when they were preparing to close their chapter, and with that all said, Me, Myself and I drove off on their way and crossed the line to the next chapter, just because they all were on their way to being happy that didn't mean that they had to forget about the lessons that they had learned before. The biggest lesson that they had learned was that they never have to forget in order to forgive, so on the start of their new journey they had their scars that didn't hurt them anymore, their souvenirs that reminded them of the lessons that they had learned, the tattoos, the poems, but the scars also reminded her what scars were too deep which were scars that she would never remake.

She went through the checklist and she had everything she needed for the next chapter, but the rest of the book was yet to come, but for now, her and her new friends for life were driving straight to their destination with a lot of pit stops in between their journey, because their journey was too long to not take as many pit-stops, but way too short to miss out. So Me, myself and I made a pact to never let life pass them by which they could easily comply with because they were 3 people in one body, and they were sure to be there for each other for every turn that they hit in the road ahead, it's not like they could go anywhere anyway because they were apart of her, but what really mattered was that they actually wanted to stay with her and finish her life's story with her, and she would meet lots of new friends along the way, but there isn't anyone out there who can replace you because you are one of a kind and we can't control people's actions but we can control ours, and that's one thing that we can always be sure of, the fact that you can always count on you if you don't know who to trust, they were all ready for the next chapter to start and they seemed to be 5 seconds away from the high road, so hopefully her journey helped you as much as it helped me, "Me, myself and I" are friends who will literally "Ride or Die" with her, so I know they will all be fine.

Printed in the United States
By Bookmasters